Dedication

I would like to dedicate this book to my children, siblings, nieces, nephews, aunties, uncles, cousins, parents, grandparents, in-laws, x-in-laws, x-wives and friends. Your love and continued patience are undeniable.

James 1: 2-3

1975 -

DIVES

VALDE

FELIX

S

PROSPERUM

Fidem Remissionem Humilitas

CopyRight@2023

Index

Chapter 1
Called To Conquer   1

Chapter 2
Destined For Greatness   14

Chapter 3
God's Masterpiece   20

CrossWord Puzzle   29

Called To Conquer

Chapter 1

"Called to Conquer"

America is being led right into the greatest catastrophe of its history and era. We are witnessing a valiant push in America to legalize sin, wickedness, and unrighteousness. It appears that the powers of darkness through legislation are seeking to normalize transsexuality, pedophilia, and perversion under the guise of human rights.

What we called sin yesterday is now called human rights, today.
The image of God and his divine order is under attack, now more than ever. The plan, plot, scheme, maneuver, and stratagem of the enemy is to remove God from homes, marriages, families, schoolhouses, church, community, government, and the nations.

When the image of God is fully destroyed and removed from hearts and minds there is no God to contend with. Now Satan and the Antichrist can appear overtly killing, stealing, tricking and destroying lives of the unsaved, saved and lost.

If you remember the sorcerer Balaam could not curse the children of Israel because they were blessed by almighty God. And he who God has blessed no man, no sorcerer, can curse. However, the children of Israel

2

could only curse themselves by turning their backs on God, his order, and his commandments. The children of Israel through disobedience and the worship of false gods, cursed themselves.

America the only person that can bless you is you. The only person that can curse you is you. The only person that can conquer you is you. To the young people and the young in heart, the only person that can curse you is you. The only person that can bless you is you. The only person that can conquer you is you. This is spiritual law, God's law.

As long as, Samson honored God's covenant he was **<u>untouchable</u>** but when he broke covenant he was turned over to his enemies. As long as, the Children of Israel honored God they were **<u>unstoppable</u>**. Balaam and Balak sorcery had no power, no effects or impact against their lives but when they broke covenant, they were turned over to their enemies.

As long as King David honored God's covenant he was **<u>unbreakable</u>** but when he broke covenant and killed Uriah to cover his adulteress affair with Uriah's wife all hell broke loose in his household.

In America, not sure if you have noticed but all hell has broken loose. Students are fighting their teachers. Teachers are sleeping with their students. Kids are raising their parents.

The earth is quaking, there are unprecedented wildfires, unprecedented tornadoes, flash-floods, tropical storms and hurricanes.

Abroad, we are on the fringes of war and we are on the verge of being turned over to our enemies. Recently, China brokered a truce, an alliance and allegiance between two arch enemies, Iran and Saudi Arabia. This deal from China's perspective was to stiffen and beef up the Middle East presence and support to dethrone the United States economic stronghold on the east.

What China was saying to Iran and Saudi Arabia is stop fighting one another. The real enemy is not yourselves or each other but the real enemy is the United States of America.

When God created us, he created us in his image. God fearfully and wonderfully made us not to be conquered but to conquer. Amid the chaos, the difficulties, and the challenges it's a dawning of new day.

We can't change where we've been, but we can change where we are going. Why? Because we have been, **"Called to Conquer!"**

In our scripture text Matthew 14th Chapter verse 22-24, we find Jesus's disciples getting into a boat, being sent into a storm, on their way to the other side. Why would God send his disciples into a storm? Let me rephrase that question. Why would God send you or I into a storm?

God knew the storm was nothing before his disciples. The storm also knew it was nothing before the disciples. The only persons who did not know the storm was nothing before them was the disciples.

My question to you is, "What is it that God knows about you that you have yet to discover about yourself?" Why is it in Genesis, Satan is a serpent but in the book of Revelations he is a dragon? Let me answer that question for you because we have fed him with our ignorance and he has grown.

There is a story about a young boy who was outside of the church and as the preacher would preach about Satan saying, Satan did this, Satan did that, the spirit in the church would get high.

The higher the spirit rose in the church the louder the boy would cry. One of the ushers inside the church heard the boy's cry outside the church.

The usher went outside and asked the boy what was wrong. He said there is just no way, I could have done all that the preacher has said. She asked the young boy what is your name? He said Satan. She said how could you not have done all that the preacher has said, "then Satan answered. I am not omnipresence, omnipotent or omniscient!"

Like the disciples many of us are ignorant to the truth. What truth? We have been, **"Called to Conquer!"**

God's purpose of Satan, our battles, hardships and storms is to cause us to look inwardly not outwardly. Look inwardly? Yes, according to Romans 8:11 that same spirit that raised Jesus from the dead dwells within each of us. It is the unconquering spirit of God.. according to Second Corinthians Chapter 2 verse 14 that always causes us to triumph, always causes us to conquer.

The unconquering spirit of God is the only weapon young people and the young at heart will ever need in life. In fact, when we accepted Christ as our personal savior we all hit the lottery, right then. But some of us don't believe that. This is why some of us still play the lottery even now.

Esoterically, according to the book of Matthew chapter 6 verse 33, when we discover who we really are in God and who God really is in us then all these things will be added unto us. Things become a never-ending gift placed under the tree of our lives. The disciples did not prefer the storm on their way to the other side or on their way to their destiny.

Like, the disciples we prefer every day to be like Sunday. We prefer not to be in a storm, not to be in hardship, not to be in trouble, not to be in a bind, not to be in a fix or even on the enemies hit list. Like Jacob, who buried his preferred Rachel on the way to destiny.

We too, on our way to destiny, on our way to class, on our way to graduation, on our way to work, on our way to the doctor's office, on our way to the lawyer's office, on our way to court, on our to the child custody hearing, on our way to the next level, and on our way through the storms of life will have to bury our Rachel.

We will have to bury our comfort levels and preferences, at the expense of what we like, dislike and ultimately prefer. Why? Because we have been, **"Called to Conquer**!**"**

The scripture says that when Peter took his eyes off Jesus he began to sink. When we take our eyes off Jesus we succumb to the peer pressure of the storm, the peer pressure of our battles, the peer pressure of our friends, and the peer pressure of the moment.

We are not too designed to succumb; we are not designed to sink. We are not designed to take our eyes off Jesus. Why? Because we have been, **"Called to Conquer!"**

- Adultery is not supposed to conquer you;

- Fornication is not supposed to conquer you;

- Homosexuality is not supposed to conquer you;

- Fear is not supposed to conquer you;

- The divorce is not supposed to conquer you;

- That bad teacher with that bad attitude is not supposed to conquer you;

- Those thoughts of suicide, depression, anxiety, loneliness and addiction are not supposed to conquer you;

- That legal issue is not supposed to conquer you;

- The mental, physical, and verbal abuse is not supposed to conquer you;

- The death of your loved one is not supposed to conquer you. Why? Because you have been, **"Called to Conquer!"**

If the storm could not conquer the disciples, if the sorcerer Balaam could not conquer God's children, if a liar could not conquer God's chosen, if a conspiracy could not conquer God's elect, if a hater could not conquer God's anointed, if death could not conquer God's appointed, then with God nothing can conquer you.

Why? Because you have been, **"Called to Conquer!"**

You are the only sign, miracle and wonder that the world will see, hear and believe in. Yes believe that if God did it for you, I know he can do it for me.

According to Psalms 31 verse 15, Not only are our times in God's hands but our storms, our challenges, and our battles are all in God's hands. And he has promised to deliver us. Why? Because we have been, **"Called to Conquer!"**

- I am here to tell you that there is a trucking company in you, a franchise in you, a school, a university, a doctor, a lawyer, a judge in you;

- I am here to tell you that there is an engineer in you, a scientist in you, an archeologist in you;

- I am here to tell you there is a Rolls Royce in you, a Bentley in you, a Lamborghini, a Helicopter, a Gulfstream G3 Private Jet in you;

- I am here to tell you there is Commissioner in you, a Mayor, a Congressman, a Congresswoman, a Governor, a Senator in you;

- I am here to tell you that there is a President, a Vice President, an Attorney General and Ambassador in you;

- I am here to tell you that there is a King, a Queen, and Priest in you.

- I am here to tell you there is an apartment development in you;

- I am here to tell you that there is a hotel development in you;

- I am here to tell you there is a builder in you, there is a new construction residential and commercial development project in you;

- I am here to tell you there is a bank in you and you shall lend to many and not borrow; I am here to tell you that God has made you the head and not the tail; I am here to tell you that God has placed you above and not beneath;

- I am here to tell that God's favor is not for a moment but for a lifetime

- I am here to tell you that weeping may endureth for a night but joy comes in the morning;

- I am here to tell you that they that sow in tears shall reap in joy;

- I am here to tell you don't get weary in doing well it is your overdue season now;

- I am here to tell you that there will be such abundance and blessings that the plowman will overtake the reapers in your life;

- I am here to tell you that no weapon formed against you shall prosper;

- I am here to tell you that no weapon formed against your family shall prosper;

- I am here to tell you that no weapon formed against your marriage shall prosper;

- I am here to tell you that no weapon formed against your business shall prosper;

- I am here to tell you that no weapon formed against your church/ministry shall prosper and every word that revolts against you, is condemned;

- I am here to tell you that Good is inside of you;

- I am here to tell you that God is inside of you;

- I am here to tell you that there is Greatness inside of you;

- I am here to tell you that Impossibility is about to honor you.

Why? Because you have been, **"Called to Conquer!"**

Destined For Greatness

Chapter 2

"You are Destined for Greatness"

All over the world there appears to be a cloud looming over the entire world. In America we are on the brink of civil war from political unrest, moral decay, gender misidentification and misclassification.

In the East, we are watching our enemies build alliances and allegiances in efforts of dethroning America's standing as the world's superpower and America's currency. Leading this coalition is Brazil, Russia, India, China, and Saudi Arabia which is where the acronym "Brics" B.R.I.C.S. has been derived.

In America, Biden versus Trump is being played out in the main stream media. We have been told a threat to our democracy is a threat to the United States of America but the greatest threat to America is not Biden or Trump. **The greatest threat to America is the truth.**

We are learning that wildfires don't burn entire areas anymore. We are learning wildfires can break out anywhere and burn your house and skip my house and burn two or three more houses and skip two or three more houses down the street.

Could it be possible that these wildfires are the results of direct energy weapons (DEW)? According to John 10:10 we know who is engineering all of this wickedness, the great liar and deceiver himself, Satan and his team of cohorts are up to their same tricks again, to steal, kill and destroy.

We are all under attack, thinking the same question. Could this be the end? Why would God allow bad things to happen to good people? Particularly why would God allow bad things to happen to God's very own people?

Joni Eareckson Tada an Evangelical Christian author, (artist, singer, radio personality, disability rights advocate) who is credited with accelerating Christian ministry in the disabled community said, **"Sometimes God allows what he hates to accomplish what he loves."**

I am here to announce that you, your spouse, your children, grandchildren, siblings, nieces, nephews, aunties, uncles, cousins, parents, grandparents and friends are not destined to failure, defeat, doom or gloom but **"You are Destined for Greatness!"**

In our scripture text First Samuel 16th Chapter verse 11 we find David, being over-looked, looked down upon, not preferred, not invited to the selection party but, **"Destined for Greatness!"**

One thing I like about God he knows how to bring the selection party to you. In Isaiah 49 verse 16, it says that our walls, (which means our hardships, battles, circumstances, situations and difficulties) are continually before God.

God knows where we are. When you are destined for greatness you don't have to go looking for promotion or elevation. Like David, promotion and elevation will find you. The bible says in Psalms 75 verses 6-7, promotion comes neither from the east, nor from the west, nor from the south but from God.

In Proverbs 21 verses 1, it says the King's heart (which means promotion and elevation) is in the hand of the Lord, he turneth it whithersoever he will.

David the little shepherd boy was destined for greatness. He was destined for promotion and he was destined for elevation. The stature of his brothers, nor the partiality of his Dad, or his inexperience could stop or alter the fact that he was, **"Destined for Greatness."**

Like many of you, the way things appear right now can not stop or alter the fact that, **"You are Destined for Greatness!"**

It doesn't matter what is happening in America's house, the white house, the congressional house, the court house, the house around corner or down the street, **"You are Destined for Greatness!"**

Unexplainable wildfires, flash floods, storms, hurricanes, partiality, injustice and a declining economy will have no effect on you. In Psalms 66 verse 12, it says that we have went through the fire and through the water, and God brought us out into a wealthy place.

No matter how faithful, crafty, and cunning Satan and his cohorts are. No matter how faithful our challenges, battles, hardships, circumstances, situations or difficulties are.

God's faithfulness will never be outmatched or out-witted. Why? Because **"You are Destined for Greatness!"** As a church body, corporately, **"We are Destined for Greatness!"**

The church is not looking for answers for we have the answer and his name is Jesus (Yeshua).

The bible is right in Romans 2 verse 11, when it says that God is no respecter of persons. I would like to submit to you that God does have favorites. Yes, God favors his children over his creation.

In Psalms 5 verse 12, is says for you, O' Lord, will bless the righteous; with favor, you will surround him as with a shield. This scripture means that God will surround his children with a shield of favor. This is why as a child of God, you are **unstoppable,** you are **unbreakable,** you are **unshakeable** because **"You are Destined for Greatness!"**

Did you know as a child of the King, a child of God, favored by God almighty and feared by the enemy, **"You are Destined for Greatness?"**

In Psalms 34 verse 7, it says the angel of the Lord encamps around those that fear him. This scripture means that the favor of the Lord encamps around those that fear him.

- This is why things are happening for you and not to you;

- This is why the odds are for you and not against you;

- This is why you are not sick but healed fighting off sickness;

- This is why you are not poor but rich, prosperous and successful fighting off poverty;

- This is why you are praying from victory and not for victory;

- This is why it is not disappointment but divine re-appointment;

- This why we are not waiting until the battle is over but like David, we are going to shout right now.

What are we going to shout right now? We are going to shout, "I am **Destined for Greatness**. In the face of adversity, in the face of the divorce, the evil, the wickedness, sickness, loneliness, the lies, shame, heartache, and the pain," I'm going to shout aloud I am **Destined for Greatness!**

In the face of my court day, in the face of being fired, in the face of not being able to pay my rent or mortgage, in the face of the doctor's report, in the face of having filed bankruptcy, in the face of having my car repossessed, I am going to open my mouth and shout, **"I am Destined for Greatness!"**

In the face of not knowing how it is going to happen next. I am going to shout right now because I refuse to settle for anything less than God's best. Why? Because **"I am Destined for Greatness!"**

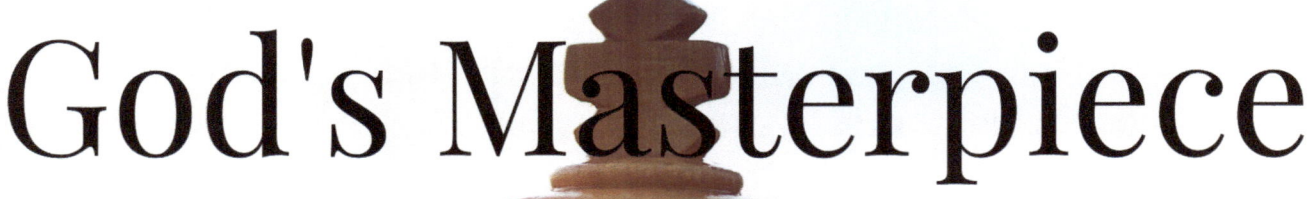

God's Masterpiece

Chapter 3

I am God's Masterpiece

I would like to examine the ministry and the flaws of God's Masterpiece. A believer is an essential part of the institution we call Church. A believer is God's gift to the church. A believer is God's gift to the community. How the church and the community treats the believer is a "thank you" gift back to Almighty God.

It has been said that to measure the impact of a church. If you remove the church from within the community does the community miss the church. I would like to submit how to measure the impact a believer has on a church. If you remove the believer from the church does the church still meet the needs of its congregants and community.

The results would conclusively reveal that every believer is **God's Masterpiece**. Why? Because every believer is an essential component of God's church and community. Without the believer there is no church and the community is doomed to hell.

The believer must be motivated by a Christ centered, unselfish love for church and community. The believer must love the work of the Lord with all his/her heart, mind, soul, body and spirit.

The believer must be able to endure and survive the bunkers, sand traps and snares of ministry. And when the believer falls down he/she must get back up again. We are talking about, **"God's Masterpiece."**

Now let's examine the flaws of God's Masterpiece. Who can find a virtuous believer? Can the board, the officers of the church. Can the research committee find a virtuous believer? A believer that is honorable that God has grown in stature and in favor with both himself and man. A believer that has been anointed and appointed by Almighty God.
Let me answer those questions for you. Only God can find a virtuous believer!
Why can God only find a virtuous believer? Because God's criterium and standard for choosing leaders is much, much different than ours.
God is not looking for a flawless believer but he is looking for a flawed believer.

In the 2nd Book of Corinthians 4th Chapter verse 7, it says that we have this treasure in earthen vessels (flawed vessels) to show that this surpassing power is from God and not from man.

I believe it was Apostle Paul that was seeking to be flawless and he asked God three times in the 2nd Book of Corinthians 12th Chapter verse 8 to remove his flaw. Apostle Paul asked God to remove the thorn from his flesh that he could become flawless.

In verse 9. God refused him three times and told Apostle Paul that his grace was sufficient. God was saying to Apostle Paul stay flawed. God is saying to you, being flawed is an honor not a dishonor in the eyesight of almighty God.

This is why in the latter of verse 9, God says to Apostle Paul that his strength is made perfect in our weakness (in our flaws) God's strength is made perfect.

In the First Book of Samuel the 13th Chapter verse 14 God said about flawed King David, he was a man after his own heart. I believe before Christ, when God looked at man he saw flaws. I believe when we have accepted Christ as our personal savior God sees Jesus when he looks at us. It is the divine presence of God, the divine power of Jesus that permeates in the life and ministry of the believer. We are no longer flawed because inside of Christ we are all flawless and inside the hand of Almighty God, **"I am God's Masterpiece"**

Approximately 40 years ago the first weekend of May 1983 there was an auction held in the Springfield community of Sparta, Georgia. The entire community was at this auction. Everyone had brought items to auction off to fundraise for improvements to the Springfield community.

At this auction there was a young violin. This violin had been looked down upon, looked over, stepped on and stepped over. This violin had no strings. This violin was deemed worthless because no one in this community really knew how to play an instrument like this.

Every other item had been sold off but this violin remained the last item unsold. The bid opened for this violin and there were no takers until one man in the crowd clothed with a garment down to his feet, his head of hair was like white pure wool, his eyes were like flames of fire, his feet were like fine brass latched inside of his saddles, his voice as the sound of many waters. It was the Son of God. He placed the violin in his hand, took the strings from his pocket, strung up this violin, tuned up this violin and began to play a masterpiece.

It was, "Amazing grace how sweet the sound that saved a wretched like me. I once was lost but now I am found. Was blind but now I can see. "

After this instrumental rendition of Amazing Grace there was one bid for $10,000.. another for $20,000.. another for $30,000.. the bidding rose to $50,000 being the winning bid. My point is, like this violin inside the hands of Almighty God, **"You are God's Masterpiece.**

Our children are God's masterpiece, our grandchildren, our siblings, our nieces, nephews, aunts, uncles, cousins, parents, and grandparents are God's masterpiece. Our businesses, our ministries, are God's masterpiece. Inside the hands of Almighty God, **"We are all God's Masterpiece!"**

And I decree and declare Isaiah 54:17 that:

- no weapon formed against your children;
- no weapon formed against your family;
- no weapon formed against your marriage;
- no weapon formed against your community;
- no weapon formed against your business;
- no weapon formed against your ministry;
- no weapon formed against your church;
- no weapon formed against the nations;
- no weapon formed against even you as a believer

shall prosper and every word that rises up against any of you is already defeated by this word of God. Why? Because inside the hands of Almighty God, **"You are God's Masterpiece."**

CrossWord Puzzle

```
U N S T O P P A B L E A B
A Z U M A M J V C D A U E
A C N A D A R A E A T N L
M A S T E R P I E C E S B
A L H A S A H A A S S H A
S L A A T A P A E E A K K
T E K A I P A N N C A A A
R E U Q N O C T A U A B E
L A B R E A A L K X A L R
A M L A D E L A B R A E B
A N E R R E A A P P A I N
U N S G D K A B L E A A U
```

CONQUER   UNSTOPPABLE   DESTINED   CALLED

MASTERPIECE   UNSHAKABLE   UNBREAKABLE   GREATNESS

Let's Pray

Father God, thank you for allowing this book to impact, activate, motivate and stimulate transformation in my life. I confess missing the mark that you have set before me. Now God I ask that you forgive me, cleanse me, renew my mind and touch even more lives as I become what has been shared in this book. I ask that you open doors that no man can close, make ways out of no ways, and make the crooked places straight in my life. Do this for me and for everyone that is connected to me, associated with me, and related to me. Destroy satan's plan against my life and detonate Christ's power, purpose and destiny in my life. Let the nations see I have been Called to Conquer, I am Destined for Greatness and I am God's Masterpiece. All these blessing and even more I ask and believe you for in the mighty matchless name of Jesus, Yeshua. Amen, Amen and Amen!

For Bookings:
Email: RichPSuccess@gmail.com

For More Books:
Visit: www.RichPSuccessful.com

www.ingramcontent.com/pod-product-compliance
Lightning Source LLC
Chambersburg PA
CBHW041557120626
46551CB00002B/243